50 WAYS WITH
RICE

50 WAYS WITH

RICE

ROSEMARY WADEY

CRESCENT BOOKS
NEW YORK • AVENEL

This 1995 edition published by Crescent Books,
distributed by Random House Value Publishing, Inc.,
40 Engelhard Avenue, Avenel, New Jersey 07001

Random House
New York • Toronto • London • Sydney • Auckland

First published by Lansdowne Publishing Pty Ltd in 1994

Managing Director: Jane Curry
Production Manager: Sally Stokes
Publishing Manager: Deborah Nixon
Project Coordinator/Editor: Bronwyn Hilton
Designed by Kathie Baxter Smith
Photography by Andrew Elton
Food Styling by Mary Harris
Printed in Singapore by Tien Wah Press (Pte) Ltd

A CIP catalog record for this book is available
from the Library of Congress

ISBN 0 517 14166 3

Front cover photograph: Lamb Biryani, recipe page 44
Page 2: Vegetarian Rice, recipe page104
Pages 8 & 9: Spiced Indian style Fried Rice, recipe page 80
Back cover photograph: Cheese and Rice Soufflés, recipe page 16

Contents

Introduction 6
Types of Rice 7
The Recipes 9

Avocado, Crab and Rice Salad 10
Brown Rice Salad 12
Cabbage Parcels 14
Cheese and Rice Soufflés 16
Cheese, Celery and Rice Galantine 18
Chicken and Mushroom Risotto 20
Chinese Chicken Broth 22
Chinese Fried Rice 24
Coconut Rice with Meatballs 26
Dolmades 28
Fennel, Salmon and Rice Salad 30
Fragrant Plum Puddings 32
Fruited Rice Ring 34
Indian-Style Rice Pudding 36
Italian Rice Salad 38
Jambalaya 40
Kouliabiaca Plait 42
Lamb Biryani 44
Milanese Risotto 46
Mushroom Pilau 48
Nasi Goreng 50
Paella 52
Pancakes with Rice and Chicken Stuffing 54
Pollo con Arroz 56
Rice Brulee 58
Rice, Chili Bean and Celery Bake 60

Rice Fritters 62
Rice Omelette 64
Rice Pilau 66
Riso con Gambero Salsa 68
Saffron Rice with Spiced Chicken Breasts 70
Salmon and Tarragon Kedgeree 72
Seafood Chowder 74
Seafood Risotto 76
Smoked Salmon and Rice Paté 78
Spiced Indian-style Fried Rice 80
Spinach and Rice Castles 82
Stir-fried Rice with Vegetables 84
Stuffed Eggplant (Aubergine) 86
Stuffed Mushrooms 88
Stuffed Peppers 90
Sushi 92
Traditional Kedgeree 94
Traditional Rice Pudding 96
Tuna and Rice Crumble 98
Vegetable Rice Loaf 100
Vegetable Risotto 102
Vegetarian Rice 104
Waldorf Rice Salad 106
Wild Rice Ring with Tuna Mayonnaise 108
Perfect Rice — Each Time: Boiled Rice, Absorption Method Rice and Microwaved Rice 110

Index 111

INTRODUCTION

Rice is healthy, nutritious, tasty, economical and easy to cook and serve. It blends well with all types of foods, sweet and spicy — including meat, poultry, fish, eggs and vegetables. As inexpensive an ingredient as you could hope for, rice is a perfect choice for budget meals. It has an excellent shelf life, both in packets (provided they are kept airtight), and in cans; and will keep in the freezer for several months.

High in nutritional value, rice is a complex carbohydrate which is digested slowly and easily by old and young alike. It is low in sodium, gluten free and contains useful amounts of the B vitamins and minerals. Brown rice especially provides a great source of energy. Rice is an important basic ingredient in vegetarian and vegan diets and in the diets of healthy-eaters of all descriptions.

There are many types of rice available each with characteristics making them suitable for particular dishes. (See page 7 "Types of Rice" for a detailed description.) Supermarkets now stock a wide variety of rice, with only the more unusual types restricted to speciality shops. Use the best-suited type of rice for your dish, as recommended in each recipe, to achieve the most delicious result.

The recipes in this book place an emphasis on quick cooking times and simple preparations to suit the busy, modern lifestyle. You can follow the three basic methods of cooking rice (see page 110) and your efforts will be rewarded with perfect, tender rice every time.

This extraordinarily versatile and interesting food produces dishes for snacks, salads, main meals, desserts and elegant entertaining involving only the minimum of time and effort. You will find recipes in this book that draw on a wealth of cooking tradition from rice-eating nations around the world: try Jambalaya, Nasi Goreng, Paella, Dolmades, Milanese Risotto or a traditional Kedgeree.

For weight-watchers, vegetarians, those who like to entertain at home, or people who simply like delicious, healthy meals that delight the eye, this book gives a selection of dishes for all tastes and occasions.

TYPES OF RICE

Aromatic Rice

The different types of aromatic rice are considered specialty rice, producing fragrance and aroma. Many are aged to increase their aromatic strength. These include:

Basmati — an extremely slender grain with both a perfumed aroma and taste which is grown in India and Pakistan and used widely in all Indian cuisine. Cook Basmati either alone or with a selection of spices to enhance it further, producing a separate and fluffy grain. A brown variety and easy-cook types are also available.

Jasmine or Thai fragrant rice a softer aromatic which can become slightly sticky unless special care is taken when cooking.

Glutinous Rice

These are sometimes called sweet, sticky or waxy rice, which accurately describes the cooked results. Japanese varieties can be used for making sushi. Chinese glutinous rice is mostly used for puddings, and the Thai varieties come in white and black grains, again mainly used for sweet recipes.

Italian or Risotto Rice

This variety of rice is used to make classic Italian risotto dishes. The grain is of medium length, stubby and able to absorb 5 times its weight in liquid while most other types of rice only absorb 3 times their weight. The best known varieties are *Arborio* and *Carnaroli* and there are also easy-cook brown and white varieties.

Long Grain or "All Purpose" Rice

The most versatile and widely used rice, originally known as "Patna" after the Indian district where it was grown. It is a long, slim grain, available as regular long grain white or brown rice; and easy-cook varieties of both (which are steamed under pressure during preparation and, therefore, virtually impossible to over cook).

Pudding or Short Grain Rice

Once known as Carolina in reference to its origins, this rice is a short stubby grain which sticks together when cooked. Used mainly to make sweet rice puddings, it is unsuitable for any spicy dish as the grains cannot be kept separate.

Wild Rice

Wild rice has long slender black grains which are often mixed with other rice to give a gourmet result that is both attractive and tasty. Wild rice is not rice in the truest sense, but the grain from an aquatic grass.

The Recipes

AVOCADO, CRAB AND RICE SALAD

*1 cup (5 oz, 175 g) fragrant Thai
    or Basmati rice*
salt and pepper
2 oranges
2 tablespoons French dressing
3 level tablespoons fromage frais
*3 level tablespoons low-calorie
    mayonnaise*
*2 oz (50 g) pecan nuts, roughly
    chopped*
*1 level tablespoon freshly chopped
    mixed herbs or half parsley and
    half chives*
4 sticks green celery, sliced
*8–12 oz (225–350 g) crab meat,
    fresh or frozen and thawed*
2 avocados
watercress to garnish

Cook the rice in salted water by any method until tender — about 12 minutes. Drain if necessary, rinse under cold water and drain again or leave until cold.

Grate the peel from 1 orange and mix with the French dressing, fromage frais and mayonnaise, and season to taste.

Cut away the peel and pith from both oranges and ease out the segments from between the membranes. Put into a bowl with the pecan nuts, herbs and celery.

Flake the crab meat roughly and add to the bowl with the dressing and mix to coat evenly. Add the cooked rice and fork through lightly, cover and leave in the refrigerator for up to 2 hours or until almost ready to serve.

Just before serving halve the avocados lengthwise, ease out the pits (stones) and carefully peel each piece. Make thin cuts into each half from the round end to the stem end but leaving a hinge. Carefully arrange the slices to form a fan by opening out. Place each fan on its own plate. Spoon the crab and rice salad over the narrow end of the fan. Garnish with watercress and serve.

Preparation time about 25 minutes

Serves 4

Brown Rice Salad

1–1 1/2 cups (6–8 oz, 175–225 g)
   brown long grain rice
salt and freshly ground black
   pepper
4 oz (100 g) green beans, topped
   and tailed
2 tablespoons French dressing
4 sticks green celery, thinly sliced
2 canned red pimientos, thinly
   sliced or 1 red bell pepper
   (capsicum), seeded and thinly
   sliced
4 oz (100 g) salted groundnuts
   (peanuts)

Mustard and Cheese Dressing:
3 tablespoons olive oil
4 teaspoons wine vinegar
1 teaspoon lemon juice
1/2 level teaspoon dry mustard
   (mustard powder)
salt and freshly ground black
   pepper
1/2 level teaspoon caster sugar or
   1 teaspoon clear honey
1 clove garlic, crushed
3 level tablespoons light cream
   cheese or fromage frais
mixed lettuce leaves to garnish

Cook the rice in salted water by any method until tender — about 35 minutes. Drain if necessary, run under cold water and drain again; or leave until cold.

Meanwhile, cut the beans into 1 inch (2.5 cm) lengths and blanch in boiling water for 2 minutes. Drain, cool and place in a bowl with the 2 tablespoons French dressing. Add the celery, pimiento, groundnuts and season lightly with salt and plenty of pepper and mix well.

Put the oil, vinegar, lemon juice, mustard, seasonings, sugar, garlic and soft cheese into a bowl and whisk well or purée in a food processor until smooth. Serve as a dressing with the salad.

When the rice is cold, fold it evenly through the salad. Arrange a bed of mixed lettuce leaves on a platter and spoon the salad on top. Alternatively, pack the rice salad tightly into a well-oiled ring pan and unmold onto the salad leaves. Fill the middle of the ring with more salad leaves.

Preparation time about 15 minutes

Cooking time about 35 minutes

Serves 4

Variation: Strips of mortadella or salami also make a good addition to this salad. Unsalted groundnuts (peanuts) or cashew nuts can be used if preferred.

Note: White rice used in this recipe cuts the cooking time to about 15 minutes.

CABBAGE PARCELS

¾ cup (4 oz, 100 g) long grain
    brown rice
8 large green cabbage leaves
1 clove garlic, crushed
1 small onion, peeled and chopped
¾ lb (350 g) lean ground
    (minced) lamb
5 oz (125 g) can water chestnuts,
    drained and chopped
1 level teaspoon ground cumin
4 teaspoons soy sauce
salt and black pepper
14 oz (400 g) can peeled tomatoes
4 tablespoons beef, chicken or
    vegetable stock or water
freshly chopped parsley or cilantro
    (coriander) to garnish

Cook the rice in salted water by any method until tender — about 20 minutes. Drain if necessary.

Blanch the cabbage leaves in boiling water for 2 minutes each, then drain.

Put the garlic, onion and lamb into a saucepan and cook gently for about 5 minutes, stirring from time to time, until almost cooked. Add the water chestnuts, cumin, 2 teaspoons soy sauce, season to taste and simmer for 5–8 minutes. Chop one peeled tomato finely and add to the meat mixture; remove from the heat and stir in the rice.

Purée or finely chop the remaining tomatoes with their juice, add 2 teaspoons soy sauce, stock, and season to taste. Transfer to a pan, bring to a boil and pour into the base of a Dutch oven (ovenproof casserole dish).

Cut the tough stalk from each cabbage leaf. Place lamb mixture on each leaf, dividing it equally between them. Fold in the sides carefully and roll up to enclose the filling.

Place cabbage parcels in the sauce, cover with a lid or foil and cook in a fairly hot oven (400°F, 200°C, Gas Mark 6) for about 30 minutes. Serve hot, sprinkled liberally with parsley or cilantro.

Preparation time about 25 minutes

Cooking time about 30 minutes

Serves 4

CHEESE AND RICE SOUFFLÉS

3/4 cup (4 oz, 125 g) long grain rice
salt and pepper
*4 oz (100 g) cheese (Chevre,
    Gruyère, Danish blue, cheddar
    etc.)*
*1 level teaspoon coarse grain
    mustard*
1 clove garlic, crushed
few drops Worcestershire sauce
*2 level tablespoons snipped chives
    or scallions (spring onions)*
2/3 cup (5 fl oz, 150 ml) milk
2 eggs, separated

Cook the rice in salted water by any method until tender — about 12 minutes. Drain if necessary.

Put the hot rice into a food processor. Cut the cheese into small cubes or grate (depending on the type) and add to the rice with the mustard, seasonings, garlic, Worcestershire sauce and chives and process until well blended. Add the milk and continue until fairly smooth, then beat in the egg yolks.

Whisk the egg whites until very stiff, beat 2 tablespoons into the rice mixture and fold in the remainder evenly.

Divide between 4 greased ovenproof ramekins or other small dishes. Stand in a baking pan and cook in a moderately hot oven (375°F, 190°C, Gas Mark 5) for 30–40 minutes until well risen and golden brown on top. Serve immediately.

Preparation time about 20 minutes

Cooking time 30—40 minutes

Serves 4

Note: These soufflés can vary widely depending on the type of cheese and mustard chosen for use — experiment with tarragon, horseradish, Dijon, etc.

CHEESE, CELERY AND RICE GALANTINE

3/4 cup (4 oz, 125 g) long grain rice
salt and pepper
6 oz (175 g) plain cottage cheese
2 oz (50 g) mozzarella cheese,
  finely chopped
1 level tablespoon chopped chives
2 tomatoes, peeled, seeded and
  chopped
2 level tablespoons sunflower seeds
1 level teaspoon freshly chopped
  basil or 1/2 level teaspoon dried
  basil
2 sticks celery, chopped
1 ripe avocado
4 tablespoons fromage frais
1 tablespoon lemon juice
fresh basil and celery leaves to
  garnish

Cook the rice in salted water by any method until tender — about 12 minutes. Meanwhile, combine the cottage cheese, mozzarella, chives, tomatoes, sunflower seeds, basil, celery and seasonings.

Line a 7 x 3 1/2 inch (18 x 9 cm) loaf pan with parchment (baking paper).

Drain the rice if necessary and while hot combine with the cheese mixture. Pile into the lined pan, pressing down well. Cool and chill with a weight on top.

Peel the avocado and discard the pit (stone) then purée with the fromage frais and lemon juice in a food processor. Season to taste.

Turn out the rice loaf and serve in slices topped with avocado sauce and garnished with basil and celery leaves.

Preparation time 25 minutes (plus chilling)

Serves 4–5

CHICKEN AND MUSHROOM RISOTTO

2 tablespoons olive oil

1 clove garlic, crushed

1 large onion, peeled and chopped

1 lb (450 g) chicken, diced

1 1/4 cups (7 oz, 200 g) long grain rice

2 1/4 cups (18 fl oz, 550 ml) chicken stock

1 red or green bell pepper (capsicum), seeded and sliced

2 sticks celery, sliced

1 level teaspoon medium (Madras) curry powder

1/2 level teaspoon ground coriander

salt and pepper

6 oz (175 g) button mushrooms, quartered

4 oz (100 g) frozen peas, thawed (optional)

Heat the oil in a large heavy-based saucepan and fry the garlic and onion gently until soft but only lightly browned. Add the chicken and continue for about 5 minutes until well sealed, then add the rice. Mix well, add the stock and bring to a boil.

Add the bell pepper, celery, curry powder, coriander and seasonings, cover and simmer very gently for 25 minutes or until almost all the liquid is absorbed. (If dry add a little more boiling stock.) Add the mushrooms and peas (if used), mix well and continue for 5 minutes until all the liquid has been absorbed.

Serve hot with a green salad.

Preparation time about 20 minutes

Cooking time about 30 minutes

Serves 4

Variation: Omit the curry powder and add 2 level tablespoons freshly chopped mixed herbs; or add 3 tablespoons soy sauce.

CHINESE CHICKEN BROTH

4 cups (32 fl oz, 1 l) chicken stock
2 small chicken quarters or 3
   chicken thighs, cooked
1/2 cup (3 oz, 90 g) long grain rice
3/4 inch (2 cm) piece fresh ginger,
   peeled and finely chopped
1/2 lemon, halved
1 fresh bay leaf
2 oz (50 g) button mushrooms,
   thinly sliced
4–6 green (spring) onions, trimmed
   and sliced
2 oz (50 g) bean sprouts (optional)
2 teaspoons light soy sauce
salt and pepper

Put the stock into a saucepan with the chicken, rice, ginger, lemon and bay leaf, bring to a boil and simmer for 15 minutes. Remove the chicken, strip the flesh from the bones, discarding skin, gristle and bones and cut the flesh into strips. Return the chicken to the pan adding the mushrooms and simmer for 5 minutes.

Add the onions, bean sprouts (if used) and soy sauce and continue to simmer for a further 5 minutes. Discard the lemon slices and bay leaf. Season to taste and serve very hot with fresh crusty bread.

Preparation time 10 minutes

Cooking time about 30 minutes

Serves 4–5

Variation: Other types of vegetables can be added to this soup as available.

Note: This soup may be cooled and chilled for up to 48 hours; or frozen for up to 2 months. It can be reheated in a microwave in individual bowls, allow 1 1/2- 2 minutes on maximum (100%) per serving.

CHINESE FRIED RICE

1 1/3 cups (8 oz, 225 g) long grain rice
salt and pepper
3 bacon strips (rashers), derinded and chopped
1 onion, peeled and chopped
4 teaspoons sunflower oil
2 eggs
1 green bell pepper (capsicum), seeded and chopped
4 oz (100 g) frozen peas, thawed
1 tablespoon light soy sauce

Cook the rice in salted water by any method until tender — about 12 minutes. Drain if necessary, making sure the rice is very dry. If time allows, lay out on a baking sheet and leave for several hours, or place in a cool oven (225°F, 110°C, Gas Mark 2) for 10 minutes. The rice grains must be separate.

Fry the bacon and onion gently in 2 teaspoons oil until crispy; then remove from the pan. Beat 1 egg with a little seasoning, pour into the pan and cook without stirring until set. Remove from pan and repeat using second egg. Cut omelettes into narrow strips.

Heat the remaining oil in the pan and fry the bell pepper for one minute, then add the cooked rice and continue for a minute longer, stirring all the time. Add the bacon and onion, strips of omelette and peas and heat through until piping hot. Add the soy sauce and adjust the seasonings. Serve hot.

Preparation time 15 minutes

Cooking time 10 minutes

Serves 4

COCONUT RICE WITH MEATBALLS

1 lb (450 g) ground (minced) lamb
1 small onion, peeled and finely
　　chopped
1 clove garlic, crushed
2 pieces ginger (1 inch, 2.5 cm
　　each), finely chopped
salt and pepper
1 egg, beaten
2 tablespoons vegetable or
　　sunflower oil
4 level teaspoons flour
1 3/4 cups (15 fl oz, 450 ml) beef
　　stock
2 level teaspoons tomato sauce
1/4 level teaspoon ground turmeric
2 level tablespoons mango chutney

Coconut Rice:
1 tablespoon coconut oil
1 1/2 cups (8 oz, 250 g) long grain
　　rice
1/4 level teaspoon ground turmeric
2 1/4 cups (18 fl oz, 550 ml) water
2 oz (50 g) unsweetened
　　(desiccated) coconut
fresh coriander leaves or parsley to
　　garnish

Combine the lamb, onion, garlic, chopped ginger and seasonings and bind together with the egg. Shape into 16–20 small meatballs.

Heat the oil in a pan and fry the meatballs until golden brown. Remove from the pan. Retain 1 tablespoon oil in the pan, stir in the flour and cook for one minute. Gradually add the stock, tomato sauce, turmeric and chutney. Bring to a boil, season well and add the meatballs. Cover and simmer for 20–25 minutes until tender.

While meatballs are cooking, prepare the rice: heat the oil in a pan, add the rice and toss until thoroughly coated. Add a pinch of salt, turmeric and water and bring to a boil. Stir in the coconut, cover the pan tightly and simmer very gently for 12 minutes until all the liquid has been absorbed and the rice is tender.

Serve the meatballs in their sauce on a bed of coconut rice garnished with coriander leaves or parsley.

Preparation time 25 minutes

Cooking time 30 minutes

Serves 4

Note: If available, use coconut oil for a richer taste.

DOLMADES

1 1/3 cup (7 oz, 200 g) long grain
    brown rice
salt and pepper
2 tablespoons olive oil
1 onion, peeled and chopped
1 clove garlic, crushed
2 level tablespoons pine nut
    kernels
2 level tablespoons sunflower seeds
1 level tablespoon freshly chopped
    dill or 1 level teaspoon dried
    dillweed
good pinch of ground allspice
8 oz (225 g) or about 24 vine
    leaves — packet or canned
1 1/4 cups (10 fl oz, 300 ml)
    vegetable stock

Cook the rice in salted water until tender by any method —
about 25 minutes. Drain if necessary.

Heat 2 teaspoons olive oil in a frying pan and gently saute
the onion and garlic until soft. Turn into a bowl and add the
pine nuts, sunflower seeds, dill, allspice and seasonings.
Mix in the rice and leave to cool.

Simmer the vine leaves in boiling water for 5 minutes then
drain thoroughly and cool.

Put a heaped tablespoon of the rice mixture on each vine
leaf and roll up neatly tucking in the edges to make a parcel.
Pack tightly into an ovenproof casserole dish. Bring the
stock to a boil, season well and add the remaining olive
oil. Pour over the dolmades, cover tightly and cook in a
moderate oven (350°F, 180°C, Gas Mark 4) for 25 minutes.
Serve hot or cold.

Preparation time 35 minutes

Cooking time 25 minutes

Serves 4–6

Variation: Ground (minced) meats such as pork or lamb can
be added to the rice before stuffing the vine leaves, and
other herbs may be used to replace the dill.

FENNEL, SALMON AND RICE SALAD

1 ¹/₃ cup (7 oz, 200 g) long grain
   rice
salt and pepper
8–12 oz (225–350 g) fresh salmon,
   cooked
1 head Florence fennel
3–4 green (spring) onions, chopped
   or 2 level tablespoons finely
   chopped onion
1 level tablespoon capers
16–20 pitted black olives
3 tablespoons French dressing
young English spinach leaves or
   lambs lettuce
2 oz (50 g) smoked salmon
   (optional)

Cook the rice in salted water until tender by any method —
about 12 minutes. Drain if necessary.

Remove the skin and bones from the salmon and flake
evenly. Trim the fennel and reserve any feathery pieces for
garnish. Chop the remaining fennel and place in a bowl
with the salmon, onions and capers. Halve most of the
olives and add to the bowl with the dressing.

Carefully mix the ingredients together then add the cooked
rice and toss gently but evenly.

Arrange trimmed English spinach leaves or lambs lettuce
on a serving dish and spoon the salad on top. Garnish with
the remaining olives, sprigs of fennel and the smoked
salmon (if used) arranged in small rolls.

Preparation time about 20 minutes

Serves 4

FRAGRANT PLUM PUDDINGS

2 1/4 cups (18 fl oz, 550 ml) milk
1/3 cup (2 1/2 oz, 65 g) pudding rice
1/2 level teaspoon ground
   cinnamon or mixed spice
2 eggs, beaten
grated peel of 1/2 lemon
1 oz (25 g) sugar
8 oz (225 g) fresh plums, thinly
   sliced
2–3 tablespoons clear honey

Put the milk, rice and cinnamon or spice into a saucepan, bring slowly to a boil, then cover and simmer very gently for about 25 minutes, stirring from time to time. The rice should be thick but with still a little liquid remaining. Cool slightly.

Beat in the eggs followed by the lemon peel and sugar.

Grease 6 deep dariole molds or small teacups and line the base of each with thin slices of plum, then cover with the rice pudding. Cover each mold or teacup with foil and stand in a roasting pan with water coming halfway up the sides. Cook in a moderate oven (350°F, 180°C, Gas Mark 4) for 50–60 minutes until set. Turn out onto small plates to serve hot and spoon a little warm honey over each. They may also be served cold; chill in the refrigerator and then turn out. Top with honey just before serving.

Preparation time about 35 minutes

Cooking time 50–60 minutes

Serves 6

FRUITED RICE RING

2/3 cup (3 oz, 85 g) short grain rice
   (pudding rice)
2 1/4 cups (18 fl oz, 550 ml) milk
1 cinnamon bark or stick
8 oz (225 g) soft fruit (grapes,
   halved and seeded, sliced
   strawberries, raspberries, sliced
   bananas etc.)
1 oz (25 g) caster sugar
grated peel of 1 orange
4 tablespoons orange juice (fresh)
1 1/2 level teaspoons powdered
   gelatine
4 level tablespoons fromage frais
fresh fruit (strawberries,
   raspberries, grapes) to decorate

Put the rice and milk into a pan with the cinnamon bark and bring slowly to a boil, stir well then cook by the absorption method (see page 110) over a very low heat, and without removing the lid, for about 25 minutes. Check that the milk has been absorbed; if not, continue for a further 5 minutes.

While the rice is cooking, line a 2 1/2 pint (1.5 l) ring pan carefully with cling film and slice the fruit.

Remove the lid from the rice and stir in the sugar and orange peel evenly, followed by half the orange juice.

Add the gelatine to the remaining orange juice and place in a microwave oven for 30 seconds or over a pan of gently simmering water to dissolve. Cool a little and stir evenly through the rice, followed by the fromage frais.

Spoon a thin layer of rice into the base of the pan, cover with a layer of sliced fruit then add another layer of rice. Add the rest of the fruit and a final layer of rice. Level the top and hit the pan on a hard surface a few times to settle the contents evenly. Chill until set.

Turn out onto a plate and surround or fill the centre of the ring with fresh fruit.

Preparation time about 20 minutes plus setting time

Cooking time about 30 minutes

Serves 4–6

INDIAN-STYLE RICE PUDDING

1 1/4 cups (6 oz, 185 g) long grain
  rice
salt
1/2 cup (4 oz, 100 g) fine white
  (caster) sugar
1 inch (2.5 cm) piece cinnamon
  bark or stick or 1/2 level
  teaspoon ground cinnamon
1 1/4 cups (10 fl oz, 300 ml) water
4 tablespoons (2 oz, 50 g) butter
4 green cardamom seeds, split open
1/4 level teaspoon freshly ground
  nutmeg
few saffron threads
3 oz (75 g) seedless raisins
1 oz (25 g) coconut strands or
  unsweetened (desiccated)
  coconut
3 oz (75 g) flaked almonds, toasted
  or 3 oz (75 g) toasted chopped
  hazelnuts
pistachio nuts, blanched and
  roughly chopped to decorate
1 tablespoon fromage frais, natural
  yogurt or cream

Cook the rice in a large pan of boiling water with a pinch of salt added for 10 minutes, uncovered. Drain thoroughly.

Put the sugar, cinnamon and water into a saucepan, heat gently until the sugar has dissolved and then boil for 2 minutes. Remove from the heat.

Melt the butter in a Dutch oven (large ovenproof casserole dish), add the rice, cardamom seeds and nutmeg, and stir to thoroughly coat in the butter. Add the sugar syrup and saffron threads and mix gently. Cover tightly and cook in a moderate oven (350°F, 180°C, Gas Mark 4) for 45 minutes.

Stir the seedless raisins, coconut and most of the nuts through the rice, cover and leave to stand for 5 minutes before serving.

To serve, top each portion with a tablespoon of fromage frais, natural yogurt or cream and sprinkle with the remaining toasted nuts and pistachios.

Preparation time about 20 minutes

Cooking time 45 minutes

Serves 4–6

ITALIAN RICE SALAD

2 cups (10 oz, 300 g) long grain
   and wild rice
salt and pepper
16 pitted black olives, halved
4 green (spring) onions, trimmed
   and sliced
1 small green bell pepper
   (capsicum), seeded and thinly
   sliced
4–6 oz (100–175 g) Roquefort
   cheese, diced
4 oz (100 g) sliced salami, roughly
   chopped
3 tablespoons French dressing
lettuce leaves
3 tomatoes

Cook the rice and wild rice in salted water by any method until tender — about 12 minutes. Drain if necessary, rinse under cold water and drain again or leave until cold.

Put most of the olives into a bowl with the onions, sliced bell pepper, cheese and salami. Add the dressing and seasonings to taste and toss together.

Mix in the rice and, if time allows, leave for 30 minutes allowing the various elements to marry.

Arrange lettuce leaves on a platter and spoon the salad into the middle. Quarter the tomatoes and arrange with the remaining pieces of black olive to garnish the salad.

Preparation time about 20 minutes (plus 30 minutes if time allows)

Serves 4

Variation: Other varieties of blue cheese may be used in place of Roquefort; or cubes of cheddar, Gouda, Cheshire etc. may be used. Use mixed lettuce leaves for a more ornamental garnish.

JAMBALAYA

2 tablespoons olive or sunflower
  oil
12 oz (350 g) lean lamb or pork
  diced
8 oz (225 g) chicken, diced
1 large onion, peeled and sliced
1 green chili, seeded and finely
  chopped
2 cloves garlic, crushed
1 green bell pepper (capsicum),
  seeded and sliced
1 red bell pepper (capsicum),
  seeded and sliced
4 oz (100 g) button mushrooms,
  quartered
1 1/4 cups (6 oz, 175 g) risotto rice
2 1/4 cups (18 fl oz, 550 ml) beef or
  chicken stock
1/4 level teaspoon ground allspice
salt and pepper
4–6 oz (100–175 g) peeled shrimp
  (prawns)
2–3 whole shrimp (prawns),
  parsley or cilantro (coriander)
  sprigs to garnish

Heat 1 tablespoon oil in a pan and fry the pieces of lamb or pork until well sealed; reserve the oil and transfer the meat to a Dutch oven (large ovenproof casserole dish). Fry the chicken in the reserved oil until browned; transfer to the Dutch oven.

Add remaining oil to the pan and fry the onion, chili and garlic until soft. Add the bell peppers and continue to fry for a few minutes then add the mushrooms and fry a further 2 minutes, stirring occasionally.

Add the rice, stock, allspice, plenty of seasonings, and bring to a boil. Simmer for 2–3 minutes. Pour into the Dutch oven, cover tightly and cook in a moderate oven (350°F, 180°C, Gas Mark 4) for 40 minutes.

Add the shrimp and a little more boiling stock if necessary. Return covered Dutch oven to the oven for 5 minutes or until all the liquid has been absorbed.

Serve hot garnished with whole shrimp and cilantro or parsley.

Preparation time 20 minutes

Cooking time 45 minutes

Serves 4

KOULIABIACA PLAIT

$^{2}/_{3}$ cup (3 $^{1}/_{2}$ oz, 90 g) long grain
  rice
1 lb (450 g) salmon filet, skinned
  and chopped
1–2 level tablespoons finely
  chopped raw onion
2 oz (50 g) cooked peas
2 oz (50 g) button mushrooms,
  thinly sliced
3 tablespoons whipping (single)
  cream or natural yogurt
salt and black pepper
good pinch of ground allspice
14 oz (400 g) puff pastry, thawed if
  frozen
2 hard-cooked (hard-boiled) eggs,
  sliced
beaten egg or milk to glaze

Cook the rice until tender by any method, drain well and either rinse under cold water and drain again or leave until cold.

Remove any bones from the salmon, combine with rice, onion, peas, mushrooms, cream, salt and pepper to taste, the allspice, and mix well.

Roll out the pastry on a lightly floured surface to a 12 inch (30 cm) square and place the salmon and rice mixture evenly down the middle leaving a 1 inch (2.5 cm) margin at the top and base. Arrange the slices of egg over the filling.

Using a sharp knife, make 11 or 12 diagonal cuts through the pastry on each side of the filling. Lightly brush the pastry edge and strips with water. Fold the top and bottom ends up over the filling and then cover the filling with alternate strips of pastry from each side to make a plait.

Carefully transfer to a lightly greased or dampened baking sheet and glaze thoroughly with beaten egg or milk.

Cook in a hot oven (425°F, 220°C, Gas Mark 7) for 20 minutes then reduce the temperature to moderate (350°F, 180°C, Gas Mark 4) and continue cooking for about 30 minutes or until golden brown and crisp. Serve hot or cold.

Preparation time about 20 minutes

Cooking time about 50–60 minutes

Serves 4–6

LAMB BIRYANI

2 ¹/₄ cups (12 oz, 350 g)
    Basmati rice
4 teaspoons sunflower or
    vegetable oil
2 onions, peeled and chopped
1 ¹/₂ inch (4 cm) piece fresh ginger,
    peeled and grated
2 cloves garlic, crushed
1 lb (450 g) lean lamb, cut into
    ³/₄ inch (2 cm) pieces
6 green cardamom seeds
6 whole cloves
1 level teaspoon ground cumin
¹/₂ level teaspoon ground
    cinnamon
1 ¹/₄ cups (10 fl oz, 300 ml)
    natural yogurt
1 ¹/₄ cups (10 fl oz, 300 ml) beef or
    vegetable stock or water
¹/₂ cup (3 oz, 75 g) raisins or
    sultanas
salt and pepper
¹/₃ cup (1 ¹/₂ oz, 40 g) flaked
    almonds, toasted
fried sliced onion rings

Rinse the rice thoroughly under cold water until the water runs clean, then if time allows soak in cold water for 30 minutes. Drain very thoroughly.

Heat the oil in a heavy-based pan and fry the onion, ginger and garlic gently until soft. Add the lamb and continue for about 5 minutes until well sealed.

Add the cardamom seeds, cloves, cumin and cinnamon then add 2 tablespoons yogurt and heat gently. Gradually add the rest of the yogurt and bring slowly to a boil. Add half the stock and bring back to a boil; simmer for 5 minutes.

Sprinkle the raisins over the meat then sprinkle the rice overall. Add the remaining water (or sufficient to just cover the rice) and season well.

Do not stir but bring back to a boil, cover tightly and cook in a moderately hot oven (375°F, 190°C, Gas Mark 5) for 30 minutes.

Serve hot, garnished with toasted almonds and fried onions.

Preparation time 20 minutes (plus 30 minutes if time allows)

Cooking time 30 minutes

Serves 4

MILANESE RISOTTO

2 pinches of saffron threads or
   good pinch ground turmeric
4 tablespoons boiling water
1 large onion, peeled and finely
   chopped
2 cloves garlic, crushed
3 oz (75 g) butter or margarine
2 1/4 cups (12 oz, 350 g) Arborio or
   other short grain Italian rice
2/3 cup (5 fl oz, 150 ml) dry white
   wine or chicken or vegetable
   stock
5 cups (40 fl oz, 1.2l) boiling
   chicken or vegetable stock
3 oz (75 g) freshly grated
   parmesan cheese
salt and freshly ground black
   pepper
freshly chopped parsley or cilantro
   (coriander) to garnish

Put the saffron into a small bowl with the boiling water and leave to soak.

In a large frying pan, fry the onion and garlic in 2 oz (50 g) of butter until soft but not browned, then add the rice and continue for a few minutes until the grains are coated and beginning to brown slightly.

Add the wine to the rice and simmer gently, stirring from time to time, until all liquid is absorbed — about 5 minutes.

Add about 2/3 cups of the boiling stock at a time, allowing all liquid to absorb before adding more, stirring well.

When all of the stock is absorbed the rice should be tender but not soft and soggy; add the saffron liquid, parmesan cheese, remaining butter and season well. Simmer for 1–2 minutes until piping hot and thoroghly mixed, ensuring that there is no excess liquid.

Remove from the heat, cover the pan tightly and leave to stand for about 5 minutes. Give a good stir and serve at once liberally sprinkled with parsley or cilantro.

Preparation time: 15 minutes

Cooking time: 30–40 minutes

Note: For a true Italian risotto made with short-grained special risotto rice, Arboria is the best rice to use. Never wash this rice before cooking. The finished dish should be moist but not soggy, and each ladelful of stock must be fully absorbed before adding the next. Don't be tempted to hurry the process.

MUSHROOM PILAU

2 1/4 cups (12 oz, 350 g) Basmati
   rice
1 tablespoon oil
2 tablespoons (1 oz, 25 g) butter,
   margarine or ghee
6–8 whole cloves
seeds of 12–16 green cardamom
   pods
3 inch (7.5 cm) cinnamon stick
10–12 oz (300–350 g) button
   mushrooms, sliced
3 cups (24 fl oz, 750 ml) water or
   vegetable stock
salt and pepper
coriander leaves to garnish

Rinse the rice under cold water until it runs clear, if time allows, leave to soak in a bowl of cold water for 30 minutes. Drain thoroughly.

Heat the oil and butter in a heavy-based saucepan and fry the cloves, cardamom seeds, and cinnamon stick for a minute or so then add the mushrooms and cook over a high heat for 1–2 minutes, stirring all the time.

Remove the pan from the heat, stir in the rice with the water and season to taste.

Bring to a boil, cover tightly and simmer very gently for 20 minutes. Do not remove the lid during cooking.

After 20 minutes, all the liquid should be absorbed; if not, continue to simmer for a couple of minutes, uncovered. Fork the rice into a warmed dish and serve hot. The cloves and cinnamon stick can be removed if they are visible. Garnish with coriander leaves.

Preparation time about 10 minutes (plus 30 minutes if time allows)

Cooking time about 25 minutes

Serves 4–6

Note: This dish makes a great accompaniment to curry dishes or casseroles.

NASI GORENG

2 cups (10 oz, 300 g) long grain
    rice
salt and pepper
2 tablespoons oil
1 large onion, peeled and sliced
2 carrots, peeled and diced
1–2 cloves garlic, crushed
1 lb (450 g) lean pork, diced
1 1/2 level teaspoons medium curry
    powder
1/2 level teaspoon ground
    coriander
1/4 level teaspoon medium chili
    powder
1 tablespoon soy sauce
1/2–2/3 cup (5 fl oz, 150 ml) water
    or beef, chicken or
    vegetable stock
8 oz (225 g) frozen peas, cooked
2 eggs
1 tablespoon (1/2 oz, 15 g) butter
    or margarine

Cook the rice in salted water by any method until tender — about 12 minutes. Drain if necessary.

Heat the oil in a pan and fry the onion, carrots and garlic very gently until soft — about 5 minutes. Add the pork and continue to fry until well sealed, then add the curry powder, coriander, chili powder, soy sauce, seasoning and stock or water. Bring to a boil, cover and simmer for about 15 minutes or until the meat is tender and the liquid is almost absorbed. Add the rice and peas and heat through; adjust the seasonings.

Whisk the eggs lightly with 1 tablespoon water and seasonings. Heat the butter in a frying pan, pour in the egg and cook gently, leaving undisturbed until set. Turn out and cut into narrow strips.

Serve the nasi goreng hot, topped with strips of omelette.

Preparation time about 20 minutes

Cooking time about 25 minutes

Serves 4

Paella

2 chicken quarters (wing or leg)
2 tablespoons olive oil
1 onion, peeled and sliced
1 green bell pepper (capsicum),
    seeded and sliced
1 red bell pepper (capsicum),
    seeded and sliced
1–2 cloves garlic, crushed
14 oz (400 g) can peeled tomatoes
2 inch (5 cm) piece cinnamon bark
    or stick
salt and pepper
1 3/4 cups (15 fl oz, 450 ml)
    chicken stock
1/4 level teaspoon saffron
2 tablespoons boiling water
1 1/3 cups (7 oz, 220 g) long grain
    rice
4 oz (100 g) peeled shrimp
    (prawns), thawed if frozen
4 oz (100 g) squid rings (calamari),
    thawed if frozen
3 oz (75 g) chorizo (Spanish spiced
    sausage), sliced
12–16 shrimp (prawns) in shells
6 oz (175 g) frozen peas, thawed
12–16 large fresh mussels,
    thoroughly cleaned, or bottled
    mussels

Cut the chicken into small pieces discarding as much of the carcass as possible. Heat the oil in a large frying pan, casserole dish or paella pan and fry the chicken and onion until golden brown.

Add the bell peppers and garlic and continue for 2–3 minutes then add the canned tomatoes and their liquid, cinnamon, seasonings and stock, and bring to a boil. Cover and simmer gently for 15 minutes until the chicken is tender.

Mix the saffron with the water then add to the pan with the rice and bring back to a boil. Cover and simmer gently for 15 minutes.

Stir in the shrimp, squid rings, chorizo, shrimp in shells and peas, and place the mussels on top. Add a little more boiling stock or water if needed. Cover again and simmer for about 10 minutes or until the rice is tender, all the liquid has been absorbed and the mussel shells have opened. (If any shells remain closed, discard them.)

Serve paella hot with crusty bread and provide a finger bowl and paper napkins.

Preparation time about 15 minutes

Cooking time about 40 minutes

Serves 4

Pancakes with Rice and Chicken Stuffing

³/4 cup (4 oz, 100 g) long grain and wild rice mixed

salt and pepper

1 cup (4 oz, 100 g) plain flour

1 egg

1 ¹/4 cups (10 fl oz, 300 ml) milk or milk and water mixed

olive or sunflower oil or shortening (lard) for frying pancakes

³/4 cup (7 oz, 200 g) fromage frais

4–6 green (spring) onions, trimmed and chopped

¹/3 cup (1 ¹/2 oz, 40 g) pecan or cashew nuts, roughly chopped

10–12 oz (300–350 g) cooked chicken, diced

1 level tablespoon freshly chopped dill or 1 level teaspoon dried dillweed

2 level tablespoons grated Parmesan cheese

Cook the rice in salted water by any method until tender — about 12 minutes.

Sift the flour with the salt and pepper into a bowl. Make a well in the middle and add the egg and half the milk. Whisk together until smooth then gradually beat in the remaining milk.

Heat a little oil or shortening in a small frying pan, pour in sufficient batter to cover the base and cook for about 2 minutes until golden brown. Turn over and cook for about one minute until browned. Make 7 more pancakes by this method, separating each with a disc of parchment (baking paper).

Combine the fromage frais, onions, nuts, chicken and dill with plenty of seasoning; then add the cooked rice and mix well.

Fold each pancake into four and divide the filling between them, spooning into one of the pockets of each. Stand in a Dutch oven (large ovenproof casserole) or dish and sprinkle with cheese. Cover with foil or a lid and cook in a fairly hot oven (400°F, 200°C, Gas Mark 6) for 30–35 minutes until piping hot.

Preparation time about 25 minutes

Cooking time about 30 minutes

Serves 4

POLLO CON ARROZ

1 tablespoon olive oil
4 chicken quarters (wing or leg) or
    8 chicken thighs
salt and pepper
4 level tablespoons paprika
1 large onion, peeled and chopped
1/2-1 green chili, seeded and finely
    chopped or a good pinch of hot
    chili powder
1–2 cloves garlic, crushed
1 red bell pepper (capsicum),
    seeded and sliced
1 3/4 cups (15 fl oz, 450 ml) chicken
    stock
14 oz (400 g) can peeled tomatoes
2 cups (12 oz, 350 g) risotto rice
parsley to garnish

Heat the oil gently in a Dutch oven (large ovenproof casserole dish). Season the chicken with salt, pepper and 2 level teaspoons paprika then brown in the oil. Remove from the pan.

Add the onion, chili and garlic to the pan and fry gently until soft, then add the bell pepper and continue for a minute or so longer.

Add the stock, tomatoes and their juice, and rice, and bring to a boil. Season well, add remaining paprika, stir well and place the pieces of chicken on top. Cover tightly and simmer very gently for 5 minutes then transfer to a fairly hot oven (400°F, 200°C, Gas Mark 6) for about 30 minutes, until the rice is tender and the liquid absorbed.

Serve from the dish, with a liberal sprinkling of chopped parsley on each portion.

Preparation time about 20 minutes

Cooking time about 30 minutes

Serves 4

RICE BRULEE

³/₄ cup (4 oz, 100 g) short grain
*   rice (pudding rice)*
2 ¹/₄ cups (20 fl oz, 570 ml) milk
grated peel of 1 lemon
good grating of fresh nutmeg
2 level tablespoons fine white
*   (caster) sugar*
2 peaches or nectarines
5 oz (150 g) fromage frais
3 level tablespoons demerara sugar

Cook the rice in the milk by the absorption method (see page 110) for about 25 minutes over a very low heat until thick and creamy, leaving a little milk in the pan. Remove from the heat and stir in the lemon peel, nutmeg and sugar.

Divide between 4–6 ovenproof ramekins or small dishes (or use one larger dish if preferred).

Quarter the peaches or nectarines, remove the pits (stones) and slice thinly. Arrange evenly over the rice. Top with a layer of fromage frais and sprinkle each with about 1 ¹/₂–2 teaspoons demerara sugar.

Put under a moderate broiler (grill) for 2–3 minutes until the sugar begins to caramelize and the fromage frais bubbles.

Serve hot or leave to cool and chill before serving.

Preparation time 10 minutes

Cooking time about 25 minutes

Serves 6

Note: Use skimmed milk or semi-skimmed milk to lower the kilojoule (calorie) count. Other fruit such as raspberries, sliced strawberries, blackcurrants, blueberries, bananas, grapes etc. may be used as alternatives.

RICE, CHILI BEAN AND CELERY BAKE

1 tablespoon olive oil
1 onion, peeled and thinly sliced
1–2 cloves garlic, crushed
15 oz (425 g) can chili beans in
    chili sauce
4 sticks celery, sliced crosswise
4 oz (100 g) mushrooms, quartered
1 1/2 cups (9 oz, 250 g) long grain
    rice
salt and pepper
2 1/2 cups (20 fl oz, 600 ml)
    vegetable stock or water
1 1/2 oz (40 g) mature cheddar or
    Gruyère cheese, grated
    (optional)

Heat the oil in a Dutch oven (ovenproof casserole dish) and fry the onion and garlic very gently until soft. Add the chili beans and their sauce, celery and mushrooms and simmer for about 2 minutes.

Add the rice, seasonings and stock, and bring to a boil; cover and simmer gently for 5 minutes.

Transfer the casserole to a moderate oven (350°F, 180°C, Gas Mark 4) for 30 minutes, until all the liquid has been absorbed and the rice is tender.

If desired, fork up the rice and then sprinkle with grated cheese and put under a moderate broiler (grill) for a few minutes until browned. Serve hot.

Preparation time 15 minutes

Cooking time 30 minutes

Serves 4

Note: Other vegetables such as bell pepper (capsicum), sliced zucchini (courgettes), carrots, fennel etc. may be interchanged with the suggested vegetables for variety.

RICE FRITTERS

1 cup (4 oz, 100 g) plain flour
salt and pepper
2 eggs
1 cup (8 fl oz, 250 ml) milk
1 1/4 cups (6 oz, 175 g) cooked
  rice (long grain, Basmati,
  brown etc.)
4 oz (100 g) cooked peas
7 oz (200 g) can corn kernels,
  drained
2 level tablespoons snipped chives
  or green (spring) onion tops
vegetable oil or shortening (lard)
  for frying
2 level tablespoons freshly grated
  parmesan cheese

Sauce:
6 tablespoons (3 oz, 75 g) fromage
  frais
2 level tablespoons snipped chives
1 tablespoon wine vinegar

Sift the flour into a bowl and season well with salt and pepper. Make a well in the middle and add the eggs and half the milk. Whisk until smooth and then slowly add the rest of the milk and continue to whisk until smooth. Add the cooked rice, peas, corn and chives.

Heat a little oil or shortening (lard) in a frying pan and add heaped tablespoons of the mixture. Cook for 2–3 minutes until golden brown underneath, then turn over carefully and cook the other side. When golden brown, drain on absorbent paper towel; put onto a plate and sprinkle each lightly with grated parmesan cheese. Serve warm.

Sauce: Combine the fromage frais, chives and wine vinegar, and mix well and serve with the fritters.

Preparation time 15 minutes

Cooking time about 15 minutes

Serves 4–5 (makes about 16 fritters)

Variation: Add diced cooked bacon, ham or poultry to the fritters. They can also be made much smaller and served cold as a snack.

RICE OMELETTE

1 tablespoon olive oil
1 small onion, peeled and thinly
   sliced
2 carrots, peeled and finely
   chopped
1 clove garlic, crushed
6 eggs
3 tablespoons water
salt and black pepper
3/4 cup (4 oz, 100 g) cooked rice
   (Basmati, long grain, brown
   etc.)
3 oz (75 g) cooked peas or beans,
   chopped
1/2 level teaspoon dried mixed
   herbs or Italian herbs
3 tomatoes, sliced
3 oz (75 g) mature cheddar cheese,
   grated

Heat the oil in a large frying pan and fry the onion, carrots and garlic very gently until soft — about 5 minutes.

Beat the eggs with the water, seasonings and cooked rice. Pour into the pan and sprinkle with the peas or beans. Cook gently until almost set, loosening the omelette around the edges as it cooks.

Sprinkle the herbs over the top of the omelette then arrange tomato slices on top and sprinkle with the cheese.

Place under a moderate broiler (grill) for a few minutes until the egg is completely set, and the cheese is bubbling and beginning to brown. Do not overcook.

Cut into quarters and serve each wedge with a salad garnish, and with crusty bread or rolls.

Preparation time about 10 minutes

Cooking time 10–15 minutes

Serves 4

Variation: Any cooked vegetables can be added to this omelette, depending on what is available or left over. Chopped meat, bacon, ham, chicken or fish can also be added. Cut the omelette into small squares to serve cold as a snack.

RICE PILAU

1 ¹/₂ cups (8 oz, 225 g) Basmati rice
2 tablespoons (1 oz, 25 g) butter or
    margarine
1 oz (25 g) blanched almonds, cut
    into slivers
1 medium onion, peeled and thinly
    sliced
1 inch (2.5 cm) piece fresh ginger,
    peeled and finely chopped
1 clove garlic, crushed
6 green cardamom seeds
6 whole cloves
2 inch (5 cm) piece cinnamon bark
    or stick
2 cups (16 fl oz, 500 ml) water
¹/₂ level teaspoon salt
¹/₂ cup (3 oz, 75 g) raisins or
    sultanas
cilantro (coriander) leaves to
    garnish
grated cheddar or parmesan cheese
    (optional)

Put the rice in a sieve and rinse under cold water until the water runs clear. Drain very thoroughly.

Melt the butter in a pan and fry the almonds until pale golden-brown. Remove almonds from the pan but retain melted butter. Add onion, ginger and garlic and cook gently until soft. Stir in the spices and drained rice and mix thoroughly until coated. Add the water and bring slowly to a boil. Stir in the salt and raisins or sultanas, cover very tightly and simmer gently over a low heat for 12–15 minutes or until all liquid has been absorbed. Remove from the heat and leave to stand for 10 minutes.

Serve garnished with the toasted slivered almonds and cilantro leaves as an accompaniment. Serve topped with grated cheddar or parmesan cheese for a tasty light meal.

Preparation time 15 minutes

Cooking time about 20 minutes

Serves 4

Note: For a slightly more Indian feel, add 1 level teaspoon garam masala with the other spices.

Riso con Gambero Salsa

10 oz (300 g) long grain rice
salt

Sauce:
1 tablespoon olive oil
1 onion, peeled and chopped
1 clove garlic, crushed
12 oz (350 g) zucchini (courgettes),
    trimmed and cut into narrow
    strips
4 tablespoons dry white wine
8–12 oz (225–350 g) peeled shrimp
    (prawns), thawed if frozen
2 level teaspoons freshly chopped
    basil or 1 level teaspoon dried
    basil
4 tomatoes, peeled, seeded and cut
    into strips
4 level tablespoons fromage frais
2 level teaspoons cornstarch
    (cornflour)
salt and pepper
fresh basil leaves to garnish
2–4 cooked shrimp (prawns) in
    shells to garnish

Cook the rice using the basic boiling method (see page 110).

While the rice is cooking make the sauce: heat the oil in a pan and fry the onion and garlic very gently until soft but not browned — about 4–5 minutes. Add the zucchini and continue for a couple of minutes, stirring well. Add the wine, shrimp, basil and tomatoes and cook gently for 3–4 minutes, stirring occasionally. Add the fromage frais and continue until well heated. Blend the cornstarch with the minimum amount of water and add to the sauce. Bring back to a boil for a couple of minutes until thickened. Adjust the seasonings and serve the sauce spooned over a bed of rice. Garnish with basil leaves and the shrimp.

Preparation time about 15 minutes

Cooking time about 15 minutes

Serves 4

Saffron Rice with Spiced Chicken Breasts

1 1/2 cups (9 oz, 250 g) regular long
    grain rice
salt and pepper
1/4 teaspoon saffron threads
2 cups (16 fl oz, 500 ml) water
Sauce:
1 tablespoon oil
1 onion, peeled and thinly sliced
3–4 boneless chicken breasts, cut
    into narrow strips
4 tablespoons dry white wine
grated peel of 1/2 orange
juice of 1 orange
2/3 cup (5 fl oz, 150 ml) chicken
    stock or water
2 level tablespoons freshly chopped
    mixed herbs or 2 level teaspoons
    dried mixed herbs
4 tablespoons natural yogurt or
    light (single) cream
fresh herbs to garnish
orange slices to garnish

Cook rice with saffron by the absorption method (see page 110).

While the rice is cooking make the sauce: heat the oil in a pan and fry the onion gently until soft. Add the strips of chicken and cook until well sealed then add the wine, orange peel, juice and stock. Bring to a boil, season and simmer until the chicken is tender and the sauce well reduced. Stir in the herbs and yogurt and reheat gently; season to taste.

Fork up the rice and serve on plates topped with the herbed chicken; or stir the chicken mixture through the rice before serving. Garnish with fresh herbs and orange slices.

Preparation time 15 minutes

Cooking time about 20 minutes (depending on type of rice used)

Serves 4

Note: For plain rice omit the saffron. You can substitute the saffron with 1/4 level teaspoon of ground turmeric, which gives a similar yellow hue but obviously a different taste.

SALMON AND TARRAGON KEDGEREE

2 cups (10 oz, 300 g) long grain
    and wild rice
1 lb (450 g) piece of fresh salmon
    filet
1 bay leaf
1/2 lemon, sliced
2 tablespoons vinegar
few black peppercorns
2 tablespoons (1 oz, 25 g) butter
    or margarine
1 large onion, peeled and chopped
4 oz (100 g) button mushrooms,
    sliced
2–3 level tablespoons freshly
    chopped tarragon or 1 1/2 level
    tablespoons dried tarragon
salt and black pepper
grated peel of 1/2 lemon
2/3 cup (5 oz, 150 ml) fromage frais
4 hard-cooked (hard-boiled) eggs
fresh tarragon

Cook the rice and wild rice together in salted water by any method until just tender — about 12 minutes. Drain if necessary.

Put the salmon into a saucepan with the bay leaf, slices of lemon, vinegar, peppercorns and sufficient water to just cover. Bring to the boil, cover and simmer gently for 10 minutes. Remove the fish from the water, carefully remove skin and bones if any, and flake. (The fish may be cooked earlier and left to cool in the water.)

Heat the butter in a frying pan and fry the onion very gently until soft. Add the mushrooms and continue for 2–3 minutes longer.

Add the tarragon to the pan with seasonings and lemon peel, then add the salmon and heat thorough. Stir in the hot rice until well mixed then add the fromage frais, mix evenly and heat for a few minutes longer.

Fork up the mixture and serve on warmed plates, each portion garnished with wedges of hard-cooked egg and fresh tarragon.

Preparation 20 minutes

Cooking time 10 minutes

Serves 4

SEAFOOD CHOWDER

1 tablespoon oil
1 large onion, peeled and chopped
2 cloves garlic, crushed
1 large or 2 small red bell peppers
    (capsicums), seeded and
    chopped
14 oz (400 g) can peeled tomatoes,
    finely chopped
3 1/2 cups (29 fl oz, 900 ml) chicken
    or vegetable stock
1 level tablespoon tomato purée
2 bay leaves
salt and black pepper
1 tablespoon wine vinegar
1/3 cup (2 1/2 oz, 65 g) long grain
    rice
4 oz (100 g) peeled shrimp
    (prawns)
1–2 level teaspoons freshly
    chopped cilantro (coriander) or
    parsley
4 whole shrimp (prawns)
fresh cilantro (coriander) leaves

Heat the oil in a large saucepan and fry the onion and garlic very gently for about 5 minutes. Add most of the bell pepper and continue for 3–4 minutes, stirring from time to time.

Add the tomatoes, stock, tomato purée, bay leaves, seasonings, vinegar and rice and bring to a boil. Cover and simmer gently for 20 minutes, stirring from time to time.

Add the shrimp and cilantro, adjust the seasonings and simmer gently for 5–10 minutes, uncovered. Discard the bay leaves. Serve hot, garnished with the remaining bell pepper, whole shrimp and cilantro leaves. Rustic bread or rolls make a good accompaniment.

Preparation time about 15 minutes

Cooking time about 30 minutes

Serves 4

Variation: Green or yellow bell peppers (capsicum) may be used to make this recipe more decorative, and a small can of well-drained sweet corn kernels may be added.

SEAFOOD RISOTTO

1 tablespoon olive oil
1 onion, peeled and chopped
1 clove garlic, crushed
8 oz (225 g) white fish filet (eg cod,
    haddock), skinned and cut into
    cubes
6 tablespoons dry white wine
2 1/4 cups (18 fl oz, 550 ml) water
    or vegetable stock
grated peel of 1 orange
6–8 scallops, quartered or
    8 oz (225 g) packet seafood
    cocktail mix
6 oz (175 g) peeled shrimp
    (prawns), thawed if frozen
2 cups (10 oz, 300 g) long grain
    rice
salt and pepper
6 oz (175 g) zucchini (courgettes),
    trimmed and thinly sliced
4 oz (100 g) green beans, topped,
    tailed and cut into
    1 inch (2.5 cm) lengths
few whole shrimp (prawns) in
    shells
1–2 hard-cooked (hard-boiled)
    eggs, sliced
parsley sprigs

Heat the oil in a pan and fry the onion and garlic gently until soft.

Add the cubed fish, wine, 2/3 cup (5 fl oz, 150 ml) stock or water and the orange peel and simmer for 2–3 minutes.

Add the scallops, shrimp, rice and the rest of the water or stock. Bring to a boil, season well and add the zucchini and beans. Cover the pan tightly and simmer very gently for 20 minutes or until all the liquid is absorbed. Adjust the seasonings and serve garnished with whole shrimp, slices of egg and parsley sprigs.

Preparation time about 15 minutes

Cooking time about 20 minutes

Serves 4

Note: 12–16 large mussels in their shells may be added to this risotto about 5–10 minutes before the end of cooking time. Remember to discard any mussel shells that remain closed after cooking.

SMOKED SALMON AND RICE PATÉ

6 oz (175 g) smoked salmon
3/4 cup (4 oz, 100 g) cooked rice
*   (any type)*
2 level teaspoons very finely
*   chopped raw onion or chives*
finely grated peel of 1/4 lemon
1 tablespoon lemon juice
salt and black pepper
pinch powdered garlic
pinch of ground allspice
4 level tablespoons fromage frais,
*   sour cream or heavy (double)*
*   cream*
mixed lettuce leaves
wedges of lemon
cucumber slices

Put the smoked salmon, cooked rice and onion into a food processor and chop very finely. Add the lemon rind and juice, seasonings to taste, a pinch of powdered garlic and allspice, and process to a purée. Add half the fromage frais, and process until smooth.

Add the remaining fromage frais and purée. Adjust these seasonings.

To serve put into a piping bag fitted with a large star vegetable nozzle and pipe into 4 whirls or squiggles on small plates. Garnish each with mixed lettuce leaves, lemon wedges and cucumber slices and serve with brown bread and butter, hot toast fingers or crackers.

Preparation time about 10 minutes

Serves 4

SPICED INDIAN-STYLE FRIED RICE

2 cups (10 oz, 300 g) Basmati rice
2 tablespoons olive or vegetable oil
   or ghee
6 whole cloves
8 green cardamom seeds
1/2 level teaspoon cumin seeds
1/2 level teaspoon ground
   cinnamon or 2 inch (5 cm) piece
   cinnamon bark or stick
3 cups (24 fl oz, 750 ml) water
1 bay leaf
1/2 level teaspoon salt

Thoroughly rinse rice under cold water until the water runs clear. If time allows, soak in cold water for 30 minutes. Drain very thoroughly and leave for 2–3 minutes.

Heat the oil in a pan, add the cloves, cardamom, cumin, cinnamon, and cook for 2–3 minutes. Add the rice, and cook for 2–3 minutes, stirring frequently.

Add the water, bay leaf and salt and bring to a boil. Cover the pan tightly and simmer very gently for 20 minutes or until all liquid is absorbed.

Discard the bay leaf, turn into a warmed serving dish and serve hot.

Preparation time 15 minutes (plus 30 minutes if time allows)

Cooking time about 25 minutes

Serves 4

Variation: Brown Basmati rice may be cooked in this way, but increase the cooking time by about 10–15 minutes. Other spices may be added to vary the taste.

Note: This dish makes a great accompaniment to other Indian dishes.

SPINACH AND RICE CASTLES

*16 large English spinach leaves,
    blanched*
*3/4 cup (4 oz, 100 g) Basmati or
    long grain rice*
salt and black pepper
*2 level tablespoons toasted pine
    nut kernels*
*4–6 bacon strips (rashers), crisply
    fried and crumbled or 4 slices
    salami, chopped*
*1 level tablespoon freshly chopped
    dill or cilantro (coriander)*
*1–2 green (spring) onions, trimmed
    and chopped*
2 hard-cooked (hard-boiled) eggs
*2 inch (5 cm) piece cucumber,
    sliced*
French dressing (optional)

Blanch the English spinach leaves for 1 minute and thoroughly drain. Cook the rice by any method until tender, drain and keep warm. Meanwhile, carefully remove any tough stalks from the spinach leaves, then use them to line four lightly oiled ramekin dishes or dariole molds.

Combine the pine nuts, bacon, dill and onions, season lightly then mix in the hot rice. Pack the mixture into the lined dishes and folding extruding spinach over the mixture.

To serve warm: turn out immediately.

To serve cold: chill and ease out of the dishes when ready.

To serve hot: stand the molds in an ovenproof dish with water about halfway up the molds, cover with foil and place in a moderate oven (350°F, 180°C, Gas Mark 4) for 20–30 minutes and turn out.

Place a castle on each plate and surround with egg wedges and cucumber. Sprinkle a little French dressing over the dish if preferred.

Preparation time about 25 minutes

Cooking time none or 20–30 minutes

Serves 4

Variation: If serving hot, try coating the castles in a béchamel or cheese sauce.

Note: This dish is a great starter or vegetable accompaniment.

STIR-FRIED RICE WITH VEGETABLES

*¾ cup (4 oz, 100 g) long grain or
    Basmati rice*
salt and pepper
*1 tablespoon sesame or sunflower
    oil*
*4 green (spring) onions, trimmed
    and sliced*
*2 carrots, peeled and cut into fine
    sticks*
2–3 sticks celery, thinly sliced
*½ small cauliflower, cut into small
    florets*
*1 bell pepper (capsicum), red,
    yellow or green, seeded and
    sliced*
*3–4 oz (75–100 g) sugar snap peas,
    trimmed*
2 tablespoons soy sauce

If using Basmati rice, rinse under cold water until the water runs clear. Cook the rice in salted water by any method until tender — about 12 minutes. Drain if necessary.

Meanwhile, heat the oil in a pan or wok and add onions, carrots and celery. Cook over a fairly high heat for 2–3 minutes, stirring or shaking the pan frequently. Add the cauliflower, bell pepper and peas. Continue for a further 2–3 minutes, stirring well.

Add the soy sauce and seasonings and then add the cooked rice. Stir until evenly mixed and cook for a further minute or two until very hot. Serve at once.

Preparation time about 15 minutes

Cooking time about 10 minutes

Serves 4

Note: The selection of vegetables can be varied to suit your taste and to make use of what is available — try bamboo shoots, broccoli, mushrooms, green beans, snow peas (mange-tout), zucchini (courgettes), baby corn etc.

Stuffed Eggplant (Aubergine)

*³/₄ cup (4 oz, 100 g) long grain
    brown rice*
salt and pepper
2 large eggplants (aubergines)
1 can anchovy filets, well drained
*4–6 green (spring) onions, trimmed
    and sliced*
*12–16 black olives, pitted and
    quartered*
*2 level tablespoons freshly chopped
    parsley or cilantro (coriander)*
2 tomatoes, peeled and chopped
1 tablespoon oil
*3 oz (75 g) mature cheddar or
    Gruyère cheese, finely grated*
*fresh parsley or cilantro
    (coriander)*
cherry tomatoes

Cook the rice in salted water by any method until tender — about 20 minutes. Drain if necessary.

Halve the eggplant lengthwise and cut out the middle leaving about a ¹/₂ inch (1.5 cm) shell. Chop the flesh and put into a bowl with the cooked rice, anchovy filets, onions, most of the olives, parsley, tomatoes, a little salt and plenty of black pepper. Mix well.

Meanwhile, blanch the eggplant shells in boiling water for 5 minutes. Drain thoroughly, brush lightly with oil, and stand in an ovenproof dish. Pile the rice mixture into the eggplants. Top each with grated cheese and add the remaining pieces of olive.

Cover with a lid or foil and cook in a fairly hot oven (400°F, 200°C, Gas Mark 6) for 20 minutes. Remove the lid or foil and return to the oven for 10–15 minutes until the cheese has browned on top and the eggplants are tender. Serve hot, garnished with parsley or cilantro and cherry tomatoes or serve cold with a little French or vinaigrette dressing.

Preparation time 30 minutes

Cooking time 30–35 minutes

Serves 4

Note: If desired, a light white or cheese sauce may be served with the eggplants.

STUFFED MUSHROOMS

4 large or 8 medium flat
    mushrooms
little vegetable or sunflower oil
salt and pepper
3/4 cup (4 oz, 100 g) long grain rice
2 streaky bacon strips (rashers),
    rind removed and chopped
8 oz (225 g) chicken livers, rinsed
    and roughly chopped
1 clove garlic, crushed
1/2 level teaspoon freshly chopped
    thyme or dried thyme
12 stuffed green olives, chopped
2 oz (50 g) mature cheddar
    cheese, grated
watercress to garnish
stuffed green olives to garnish

Lightly brush the mushrooms with oil, season and stand in a shallow baking pan or ovenproof dish; leave to stand.

Cook the rice by any method in salted water until tender — about 12 minutes; drain if necessary.

Heat 1 tablespoon oil in a pan and fry the bacon, chicken livers and garlic for 4–5 minutes until tender. Add the thyme and stuffed olives and season to taste. Stir in the rice and then use to fill the mushrooms, piling up the stuffing as necessary. Sprinkle with grated cheese and cook in a fairly hot oven (400°F, 200°C, Gas Mark 6) for about 25 minutes or until the mushrooms are tender and the cheese lightly browned. Serve hot, garnished with watercress and stuffed olives.

Preparation time 20 minutes

Cooking time about 25 minutes

Serves 4 (or 8 as a starter)

STUFFED PEPPERS

1¹/₄ cup (6 oz, 175 g) long grain
   and wild rice mixed
1 tablespoon walnut oil
1 onion, peeled and chopped
1 clove garlic, crushed (optional)
1 carrot, peeled and cut into
   narrow strips
2 sticks celery, chopped
3–4 lean bacon strips (rashers),
   rind removed and chopped
   (optional)
¹/₂ cup (2 oz, 50 g) walnut pieces
1–2 level tablespoons freshly
   chopped cilantro (coriander)
   or mint
salt and pepper
4 large red bell peppers (capsicums)
2 cups (10 fl oz, 300 ml) boiling
   vegetable or meat stock
Sauce:
2 tablespoons (1 oz, 25 g) butter or
   margarine
1 clove garlic, crushed
¹/₄ cup (1 oz, 25 g) flour
²/₃ cup (5 fl oz, 150 ml) milk or
   stock
²/₃ cup (5 fl oz, 150 ml) natural
   yogurt
1 level teaspoon French or Dijon
   mustard
watercress to garnish

Cook the long grain and wild rice together in salted water by any method until tender — about 12 minutes. Drain if necessary.

Heat the oil in a pan and fry the onion, garlic, carrot, and celery for 2–3 minutes until beginning to soften. Add the bacon, if used, and continue frying until sealed. Remove from the heat and mix in the rice, walnuts, cilantro and season well.

Slice the tops off the bell peppers and reserve them. Carefully seed and stand the peppers in an Dutch oven (ovenproof casserole dish). Spoon in the rice mixture. Pack tightly, piling up the mixture and replace the tops.

Season the stock, add to the casserole and cover tightly with a lid or foil. Cook in a fairly hot oven (400°F, 200°C, Gas Mark 6) for 35–40 minutes until tender.

To make the sauce: melt the butter and fry the garlic for 1–2 minutes. Stir in the flour and cook for one minute then gradually add the milk or stock followed by the yogurt and bring slowly to a boil. Simmer for 2 minutes. Season to taste and stir in the mustard. Any juices from the bell peppers may be added.

Serve the bell peppers garnished with watercress together with the sauce for a dressing.

Preparation time 20 minutes

Cooking time 30–40 minutes

Serves 4

SUSHI

2 1/4 cups (12 oz, 350 g) short grain
    (pudding) rice
4 cups (32 fl oz, 1l) water
1/2 cup (4 fl oz, 120 ml) rice
    vinegar or cider vinegar
1–2 level teaspoons salt
2 level teaspoons sugar
1 level teaspoon ground ginger or
    ground horseradish
thin slices of raw or smoked fish
    (mackerel, salmon etc.)
salad leaves, vegetables and fresh
    herbs for garnish

Optional garnishes:
1 lemon or lime, sliced
few shrimp (prawns)
few scallops
caviar or red fish roe
carrot, grated
2–3 radishes, sliced

Soak the rice in cold water for 3 hours if time allows, otherwise rinse thoroughly under cold running water until the water runs clear. Drain very thoroughly. Put the rice and water into a saucepan and bring to a boil. Cover and simmer over a very gentle heat for about 20–25 minutes, until all the water has been completely absorbed. At this stage, the rice should still be quite firm but not hard.

Turn into a bowl and add the vinegar, salt and sugar. Mix gently then cover and put aside until cold.

With wet hands shape the rice into oval cakes approximately 1 1/2–2 inches (4–5 cm) in length. Blend the ground ginger or horseradish with the minimum of water to make a paste and then spread a very sparing layer over each rice cake.

Top each with a thin slice or twist of raw fish, shrimp or scallop. Arrange the sushi on flat platters and garnish each with pieces or twists of lemon or lime, small amounts of caviar or red lumpfish roe, grated carrot, radish slices, fresh sprigs of herbs etc.

Chill until ready to serve.

Preparation time about 30 minutes (plus 3 hrs if time allows)

Cooking time about 30 minutes

Makes approx 25–30

TRADITIONAL KEDGEREE

2 cups (12 oz, 350 g) long grain
   rice
salt and freshly ground pepper
4 eggs hard-cooked (hard-boiled)
1 lb (450 g) smoked haddock or
   cod fillets
1 1/4 cups (10 fl oz, 300ml) water
   or equal parts water and milk
2 tablespoons (1 oz, 25 g) butter
   or margarine
1 large onion, peeled and chopped
2 sticks celery, chopped
3 level tablespoons freshly chopped
   parsley
2 tablespoons whipping (single)
   cream
4 tablespoons natural yogurt
parsley sprigs to garnish

Cook the rice in salted water by any method until tender — about 12 minutes. Drain if necessary.

Poach the fish in the minimum of water, or water and milk mixed, until tender — about 5–8 minutes. Strain the fish, remove the skin and bones; flake and keep warm.

Melt the butter in a pan and fry the onion and celery very gently until soft, about 10 minutes, stirring to prevent browning. Add the flaked fish and heat through gently, then add the rice, parsley, three chopped eggs and plenty of seasonings. Heat through for 3–4 minutes, stirring carefully, until piping hot. The cream and yogurt should be mixed together and then either stirred through the kedgeree or spooned on top just before serving.

Turn the kedgeree into a warmed serving dish and garnish with the remaining egg cut into slices or wedges and parsley sprigs. Serve hot.

Preparation time about 20 minutes

Cooking time about 20 minutes

Serves 4

Variation: Fried sliced mushrooms or a tablespoon of capers or chopped dill pickles (gherkins) may be added, but this compromises the traditional taste. The kedgeree may be left to cool and each portion reheated on a plate in a microwave set on maximum (100%) for 1–1 1/2 minutes.

TRADITIONAL RICE PUDDING

3 oz (75 g) pudding rice
3 1/2 cups (30 fl oz, 900 ml) milk
3–4 level tablespoons sugar
(depending on taste)
3 fresh bay leaves or 1/2 level
teaspoon freshly grated nutmeg
2 tablespoons (1 oz, 25 g) butter or
margarine

Put the rice into an ovenproof dish with the milk, sugar, bay leaves or nutmeg and butter. Mix well.

Cook, uncovered, in a cool oven (300°F, 150°C, Gas Mark 2) for 30 minutes.

Stir the rice well and then return to the oven for a further 1 1/2-1 3/4 hours until thick and creamy and a golden brown skin has formed on top.

Serve hot as it is or with brown sugar, jam and/or cream or natural yogurt.

This pudding can also be cooked in a saucepan on the stove. Put the rice, milk and spices into a heavy-based pan and bring slowly just to a boil.

Stir well then cover tightly and simmer very gently for about 35–40 minutes, mixing from time to time until thick and creamy but not solid. Stir in the sugar to taste and butter and serve.

Preparation time 5 minutes

Cooking time approx 2 hours (or 40 minutes)

Serves 4–6

Variation: Try adding the grated peel of 2 oranges; 1 tablespoon rose water; 2 oz (50 g) raisins and 1 level teaspoon ground cinnamon or mixed spice for a fragrant and tasty pudding.

TUNA AND RICE CRUMBLE

1 cup (8 oz, 225 g) long grain rice
  (white or brown)
salt and pepper
2 tablespoons (1 oz, 25 g) butter
  or margarine
¹/₄ cup (1 oz, 25 g) flour
1 cup (9 fl oz, 275 ml) milk
1 tablespoon wine vinegar
6 green (spring) onions, trimmed
  and sliced
7 oz (200 g) can corn kernels,
  drained
1 level tablespoon capers
14 oz (400 g) can tuna chunks in
  brine, drained
2 level tablespoons freshly chopped
  mixed herbs (optional)
3 tomatoes
3 oz (75 g) mozzarella cheese,
  thinly sliced
2 level tablespoons grated
  parmesan cheese
fresh herbs or parsley to garnish

Cook the rice by any method in salted water until tender — about 12 minutes. (20 minutes for brown rice). Drain if necessary.

Meanwhile heat the butter in a pan, stir in the flour and cook for about one minute. Gradually add the milk and bring to a boil, stirring frequently; simmer for 2 minutes. Remove from the heat and stir in the vinegar and seasonings to taste, onions, corn, capers and finally the chunks of tuna.

Turn into an ovenproof casserole dish. Mix the herbs (if used) with the cooked rice and spoon evenly over the tuna mixture.

Arrange the tomatoes over the rice then add slices of mozzarella cheese and finally sprinkle with Parmesan cheese.

Cook in a fairly hot oven (400°F, 200°C, Gas Mark 6) for about 30 minutes or until piping hot and browned. Serve hot, garnished with fresh herbs.

Preparation time about 20 minutes (30 minutes for brown rice)

Cooking time about 30 minutes

Serves 4–5

Note: This dish can be prepared earlier in the day and when ready to cook from cold, put into the oven for 45 minutes. It may also be frozen for up to 2 months. Thaw completely before recooking.

VEGETABLE RICE LOAF

³/4 cup (4 oz, 100g) brown long
*   grain rice (or white rice)*
salt and pepper
4 oz (100 g) mushrooms
2 tablespoons (1 oz, 25 g) butter or
*   margarine*
1 clove garlic, crushed
1 onion, peeled and chopped
2 sticks celery, thinly sliced
2 oz (50 g) cooked peas (optional)
2 tablespoons soy sauce
2 eggs, beaten
4 oz (100 g) broccoli, trimmed and
*   blanched*
2 hard-cooked (hard-boiled) eggs,
*   shelled*
cooked baby corn to garnish
cherry tomatoes to garnish

Cook the rice in salted water by any method until tender — about 25 minutes. Drain if necessary.

Meanwhile, line a 1 lb (500 g) loaf tin with non-stick baking paper. Slice several mushrooms and pick out even-sized slices, arranging them in the base of the tin in a line. Chop the trimmings and the rest of the mushrooms.

Melt the butter and fry the garlic, onion and celery gently until soft but not browned. Add the remaining mushrooms and continue for a couple of minutes then stir in the peas (if used) cooked rice, plenty of seasonings, soy sauce and beaten eggs until well mixed.

Spoon half the rice mixture into the tin over the mushroom base. Roughly chop the broccoli and arrange in the tin with the whole eggs, and then cover with the remaining rice mixture. Level the top pressing it down evenly and firmly. Cover with a piece of greased foil and cook in a fairly hot oven (400°F, 200°C, Gas Mark 6) for 30–40 minutes or until firm to the touch.

To serve hot: turn out carefully and garnish with the corn cobs and tomatoes.

To serve cold: cool then chill thoroughly before turning out. Serve in slices.

Preparation time about 30 minutes

Cooking time 30–40 minutes

Serves 4–6

Variation: Try adding herbs to the loaf — allow 1 level tablespoon fresh herbs or 1 level teaspoon dried herbs.

VEGETABLE RISOTTO

2 tablespoons oil
1 large onion, peeled and chopped
1–2 cloves garlic, crushed
   (optional)
2 cups (10 oz, 300 g) long grain
   brown rice
3 1/2 cups (30 fl oz, 850 ml)
   vegetable stock
2 large carrots, peeled and cut into
   sticks
1 head Florence fennel, trimmed
   and chopped
4 level tablespoons sunflower seeds
salt and black pepper
1 bay leaf
1/2 level teaspoon ground allspice
2 level tablespoons freshly chopped
   mixed herbs
4 oz (100 g) button mushrooms,
   sliced
4 oz (100 g) frozen peas, thawed
   (optional)
fresh mixed herbs to garnish
freshly grated parmesan cheese to
   garnish

Heat the oil in a pan and gently fry the onion and garlic until soft. Add the rice and continue for 2 minutes, stirring frequently, then add the stock and bring to a boil.

Add the carrots, fennel, 3 tablespoons sunflower seeds, seasonings, bay leaf and allspice; cover and simmer gently for 30 minutes, without lifting the lid, or until the rice is nearly tender and most of the liquid has been absorbed.

Add the herbs, mushrooms and peas, mix well, re-cover and simmer for a further 10 minutes or until the vegetables are tender and all the liquid has been absorbed.

Serve each portion sprinkled with the remaining sunflower seeds and parmesan cheese, garnished with fresh herbs.

Preparation time about 15 minutes

Cooking time about 40 minutes

Serves 4–5

Note: White long grain rice when used in this recipe cuts the cooking time by 10 minutes.

VEGETARIAN RICE

9 oz (250 g) regular long grain rice
salt and pepper
2 cups (16 fl oz, 500 ml) boiling
    water
1 tablespoon sunflower or
    vegetable oil
1 clove garlic, crushed
4 green (spring) onions, trimmed
    and sliced
4 oz (100 g) button mushrooms
    (champignons), quartered
6 oz (175 g) carrots, peeled and
    diced
1 red bell pepper (capsicum),
    seeded and sliced
4 oz (100 g) peas or zucchini
    (courgettes), trimmed and
    thinly sliced

Cook the rice using the basic microwave method (see page 110).

While the rice is cooking, heat the oil in a pan and fry the garlic, onions, mushrooms, carrots and bell pepper for a few minutes until they begin to soften, then add the peas or zucchini and continue for a minute or so longer. Season well. When the rice is cooked stir the vegetables evenly through the rice (all the liquid should be absorbed), re-cover and return to the microwave for 1 minute. Leave to stand for
10 minutes then serve.

Preparation time 10 minutes

Cooking time about 15 minutes

Serves 4

Note: For plain rice simply cook for 10 minutes then leave to stand for 10 minutes.

WALDORF RICE SALAD

*3/4 cup (4 oz, 100 g) long grain rice
(brown or white)*
*1/2 level teaspoon ground
cinnamon*
6 whole cloves
salt and pepper
2 tablespoons lemon juice
2 red-skinned dessert apples
1 green-skinned dessert apple
3 tablespoons French dressing
*4 tablespoons thick mayonnaise or
low-calorie mayonnaise*
*6 green (spring) onions, trimmed
and sliced*
*1/3–2/3 cup (2–3 oz, 50–75 g)
walnut pieces or pecan halves,
roughly chopped*
2 oz (50 g) raisins or sultanas
*3–4 sticks celery, trimmed and
sliced*
celery leaves
watercress

Cook the rice until tender by any method with the cinnamon, cloves and a pinch of salt added — about 12 minutes for white rice or 20 minutes for brown rice. Drain rice and rinse under cold water, or leave until cold. Discard the cloves.

Put the lemon juice into a bowl. Core and slice the apples into the lemon juice, toss thoroughly.

Mix the dressing with the mayonnaise then add the onions, walnuts, raisins and celery. Drain the apples and fold into the mixture with the cooked rice.

Turn the well-mixed salad onto a serving platter or into a bowl and garnish with celery leaves and watercress sprigs.

Preparation time about 20 minutes

Serves 4–6

Variation: Other types of nuts may be used, as well as fruit such as pineapple, peaches, nectarines, and grapes. To cut calories, use a low-calorie mayonnaise mixed with natural yogurt or fromage frais in place of the French dressing.

WILD RICE RING
WITH TUNA MAYONNAISE

2 cups (10 oz, 300 g) long grain
    and wild rice mixed
salt and pepper
2 level tablespoons freshly chopped
    mixed herbs or 2 level teaspoons
    dried mixed herbs
2 tablespoons French dressing
Tuna mayonnaise:
4 level tablespoons low-calorie
    mayonnaise
4 level tablespoons natural yogurt
    or fromage frais
3/4–1 level teaspoon medium
    (Madras) curry powder
salt and pepper
3 inch (7.5 cm) piece cucumber,
    chopped
3–4 sticks celery, chopped or sliced
1 avocado, peeled, seeded and
    diced
1 level tablespoon snipped chives
    (optional)
7 oz (200 g) can tuna in brine,
    drained
watercress to garnish
celery leaves to garnish

Cook the rice and wild rice in salted water by any method until tender — about 12 minutes. Drain thoroughly if necessary. While still hot mix in the chopped herbs and dressing and pack tightly into a well-oiled 32 fl oz (1 l) ring tin. Cool then chill.

Combine the mayonnaise and yogurt, and beat in the curry powder with seasonings to taste. Add the cucumber, celery, avocado and chives (if used) and mix well. Flake the tuna fish into smallish chunks and fold carefully into the mayonnaise mixture.

Before serving, turn the rice ring out carefully onto a flat dish. Spoon the tuna mixture into the middle. Garnish with sprigs of watercress and celery leaves.

Preparation time about 25 minutes plus chilling

Serves 4

Variation: Replace the tuna with 6 oz (175 g) diced cooked ham, gammon or chicken meat.

PERFECT RICE — EACH TIME

BOILED RICE

1 1/2 cups (9 oz, 250 g) regular long grain white rice
1/2 level teaspoon of salt

Rinse rice thoroughly in a seive under cold water until the water runs clear. Drain thoroughly.

Fill a saucepan to 3/4 full with water, add salt and bring to a boil. Add rice and bring back to a boil, stirring well to separate the grains. Simmer gently, uncovered, for 12 minutes. Test: If the rice separates cleanly and is not hard in the middle, it is ready. Drain thoroughly — rinsing is unnecessary as excess starch was washed away prior to cooking.

Boiling times using above quantities:
    Regular long grain, brown — 35 minutes
    Basmati, white — 10–12 minutes
    Basmati, brown — 25 minutes
    Risotto rice — 20 minutes
    Short grain (pudding) — 40 mintues
    Long grain mixed with wild rice — 12–18 minutes

ABSORPTION METHOD RICE

1 1/2 cups (9 oz, 250 g) regular long grain white rice
1/4 level teaspoon of salt
2 cups (18 fl oz, 500ml) water

Rinse rice thoroughly in a seive under cold water until the water runs clear. Drain thoroughly.

In a saucepan with a cover that makes a secure seal, place the rice, salt and water. Bring up to a boil, stir well, cover, and cook over a gentle heat for 12 minutes. When cooked the water should be absorbed and the rice tender. Do not uncover while cooking or the steam will escape and spoil the rice.

Absorption times for 1 1/2 cups rice:
    Regular long grain, brown— 2 1/2 cups
        (20 fl oz, 625 ml) water for 35 minutes
    Basmati, white — 1 3/4 cups (15 fl oz, 450 ml)
        water for 10 minutes
    Basmati, brown — 2 1/2 cups (20 fl oz, 600 ml)
        water for 25 minutes
    Risotto rice — 4 cups (32 fl oz, 1l) water
        for 20 minutes
    Short grain (pudding) — 2 1/2 cups
    (20 fl oz, 600 ml) milk for 40 mintues

MICROWAVED RICE

1 1/2 cups (9 oz, 250 g) regular long grain white rice
1/4 level teaspoon of salt
2 cups (18 fl oz, 500ml) boiling water

Rinse the rice thoroughly in a seive under cold water until the water runs clear. Drain thoroughly. Place rice, salt and boiling water in a microwave-proof (non-metallic) bowl. Stir well, cover, and cook in the microwave on maximum (100%) for 10 minutes using a 650-watt model. (Timed will vary slightly with different wattage models — allow an extra minute for lower wattage and a minute less for higher wattage microwaves.) Leave to stand for 10 minutes.

Microwave times for 1 1/2 cups rice:
    Regular long grain, brown — 2 1/2 cups
        (20 fl oz, 625 ml) boiling water for 25 minutes
    Basmati, white — 1 3/4 cups (15 fl oz, 450 ml)
        boiling water for 8 minutes
    Basmati, brown — 2 1/2 cups (20 fl oz, 600 ml)
        boiling water for 16 minutes
    Long grain mixed with wild rice — 2 3/4 cups
        (25 fl oz, 700 ml) boiling water for 13 minutes

INDEX

absorption method rice 110
Arborio rice 7, 46
aromatic rice 7
aubergine *see* eggplant
avocado, crab and rice salad 10

Basmati rice 7, 10, 44, 48, 62, 64, 66, 80, 82, 84
bell peppers *see* peppers
boiled rice 110
brown long grain rice 14, 28, 62, 64, 86, 100, 102, 106
    brown rice salad 12

cabbage parcels 14
capsicums *see* peppers ways
Carnaroli rice 7
Carolina rice 7
celery
    cheese, celery and rice galantine 18
    rice, chili bean and celery bake 60
cheese
    cheese and rice soufflés 16
    cheese, celery and rice galantine 18
chicken
    chicken and mushroom risotto 20
    Chinese chicken broth 22
    pancakes with rice and chicken stuffing 54
    pollo con arroz 56
    saffron rice with spiced chicken breasts 70
chili beans
    rice, chili bean and celery bake 60
Chinese chicken broth 22
Chinese fried rice 24
chowder, seafood 74
coconut rice with meatballs 26
cooking methods for rice 110
crab
    avocado, crab and rice salad 10

dolmades 28

eggplant, stuffed 86

English spinach *see* spinach

fennel, salmon and rice salad 30
fish *see* seafood
fried rice
    Chinese 24
    spiced Indian-style 80
fritters, rice 62
fruited rice ring 34

glutinous rice 7

Indian-style fried rice, spiced 80
Indian-style rice pudding 38
Italian rice 7, 46
Italian rice salad 38

jambalaya 40
Jasmine rice 7, 10

kedgeree
    salmon and tarragon 72
    traditional 94
kouliabiaca plait 42

lamb biryani 44
long grain rice 7, 10, 16, 18, 20, 22, 24, 26, 30, 36, 42, 50, 52, 60, 68, 70, 74, 76, 82, 84, 88, 94, 98, 104
    with wild rice 38, 54, 72, 90, 108
    see also brown long grain rice

meatballs
    coconut rice with meatballs 26
microwaved rice 110
Milanese risotto 46
mushroom pilau 48
mushrooms
    chicken and mushroom risotto 20
    stuffed 88

nasi goreng 50

omelette, rice 64

paella 52
pancakes with rice and chicken stuffing 54
paté, smoked salmon and rice 78
Patna rice 7
peppers, stuffed 90
pilau
    mushroom 48
    rice 66
plum puddings, fragrant 32
pollo con arroz 56
prawns *see* shrimp
pudding rice 7, 32, 34, 58, 92, 96
puddings
    fragrant plum puddings 32
    Indian-style rice pudding 36
    traditional rice pudding 96

rice brulee 58
rice, chili bean and celery bake 60
rice fritters 62
rice omelette 64
rice pilau 66
rice pudding, traditional 96
riso con gambero salsa 68
risotto
    chicken and mushroom 20
    Milanese 46
    seafood 76
    vegetable 102
risotto rice 7, 40, 56

saffron rice with spiced chicken breasts 70
salad
    avocado, crab and rice salad 10
    brown rice salad 12
    fennel, salmon and rice salad 30
    Italian rice salad 38
    Waldorf rice salad 106

salmon
    fennel, salmon and rice salad 30
    salmon and tarragon kedgeree 72
    smoked salmon and rice paté 78
seafood
    seafood chowder 74
    seafood risotto 76
    sushi 92
    traditional kedgeree 94
    see also salmon; shrimp; tuna
short grain rice 7, 34, 46, 58, 92
shrimp
    riso con gambero salsa 68
smoked salmon and rice paté 78
soufflés, cheese and rice 16
soup
    Chinese chicken broth 22
    seafood chowder 74
spinach and rice castles 82
stir-fried rice with vegetables 84
sushi 92

tarragon
    salmon and tarragon kedgeree 72
Thai rice 7
tuna
    wild rice ring with tuna mayonnaise 108
    tuna and rice crumble 98

vegetables
    stir-fried rice with vegetables 84
    vegetable rice loaf 100
    vegetable risotto 102
vegetarian rice 104
vine leaves
    dolmades 28

Waldorf rice salad 106
wild rice 7, 38, 54, 72, 90, 108
    wild rice ring with tuna mayonnaise 108